# Biographies for Human Development

*to accompany*

Berk

## Child Development
## Infants, Children, and Adolescents
## Development Through the Lifespan

Prepared by

Susan Messer, Judy Ashkenaz,
*and*
Laura E. Berk

PEARSON

Boston    New York    San Francisco
Mexico City    Montreal    Toronto    London    Madrid    Munich    Paris
Hong Kong    Singapore    Tokyo    Cape Town    Sydney

ISBN: 0-205-46880-2

Printed in the United States of America

10 9 8 7 6 5 4 3 2 1       09   08   07   06   05

# CONTENTS

# BIOGRAPHIES FOR HUMAN DEVELOPMENT

*Biographies can accompany the following suggested chapters.*

| Developmental Theorist | *Child Development,* 7th edition | *Infants, Children, and Adolescents,* 5th edition | *Development Through the Lifespan,* 3rd edition |
|---|---|---|---|
| Erik H. Erikson (1902–1994) | Chapters 1, 11 | Chapters 1, 16 | Chapters 1, 12 |
| James Mark Baldwin (1861–1934) | 1 | 1 | 1 |
| Uri Bronfenbrenner (1917–) | 1 | 1, 2 | 1, 2 |
| Esther Thelen (1941–2004) | 4 | 5 | 4 |
| Eleanor Gibson (1910–2002) | 4 | 5 | 4 |
| Donald O. Hebb (1904–1985) | 5 | 5 | 4 |
| Jean Piaget (1896-1980) | 6 | 6, 9, 12, 15 | 5, 7, 9, 11 |
| Lev Vygotsky (1896–1934) | 6 | 6, 9 | 5, 7 |
| Robbie Case (1944–2000) | 7 | 9, 12, | 9 |
| Howard Gardner (1943–) | 8 | 9, | 9 |
| Fraser Mustard (1927–) | 1, 8 | 1, 2, 5, 9 | 1, 2, 4, 7 |
| Elizabeth Bates (1947–2003) | 9 | 6 | 5 |
| Jerome Kagan (1929–) | 10 | 7 | 6 |
| Mary Ainsworth (1913–1999) | 10 | 7 | 6 |
| Lawrence Kohlberg (1927–1987) | 12 | 16 | 12 |
| Albert Bandura (1925–) | 12 | 10 | 8 |
| Eleanor Maccoby (1917–) | 13, 14 | 10, 13 | 8, 10 |

# ERIK ERIKSON

Erik Homburger Erikson was born in 1902 near Frankfurt, Germany. Questions of identity clouded his early life and may well have provided the impetus for his lifelong focus on human identity and identity formation. Erikson's mother, Karla Abrahamsen, became pregnant with Erik as the result of an extramarital affair; during her pregnancy, her marriage broke up, and Erik never knew either his birth father or his mother's first husband. When he was 3 years old, his mother married Theodor Homburger, a pediatrician who had treated young Erik. Only when he reached adolescence did Erik learn that Homburger was not his biological father.

The experience of being a stepson became central to Erikson's view of himself: As the writer of his obituary in the *American Psychologist* described it, he saw himself as "a person whose presence is not justified by the usual credentials." When he moved to the United States in the 1930s, he took the name Erikson, meaning "son of Erik"—perhaps indicating his sense that the roots of his true identity lay only within himself.

After graduating from high school in Germany, Erikson enrolled in art school, but he soon became dissatisfied with the course of study. He dropped out and traveled in Europe, sketching children to earn a meager living and reading widely on his own. Then, in 1927, a friend invited him to Vienna to teach in a progressive school. In Vienna, Erikson met Anna Freud, who, seeing his potential to become a child analyst, invited him to begin psychoanalysis with her. In this way, Erikson became involved with the Viennese psychoanalytic community, and his life path began to take shape: He met and married Joan Serson, an artist and dancer who became his lifelong partner; he underwent training in child analysis in a seminar led by Anna Freud; and he gained membership in the International Psychoanalytic Association, which later made him eligible for the American Psychoanalytic Association.

As the political climate of Europe in the 1930s became increasingly threatening, many psychoanalysts left for America. Erikson and his wife emigrated in 1934 and settled in Boston. As Boston's only child analyst, Erikson was widely consulted, and he became associated with both Harvard Medical School and Massachusetts General Hospital. Between 1934 and 1936, he conducted studies of college students at Harvard's psychological clinic. The material from these studies became the background for his work on American youth, identity formation, and "identity crisis"—a term that he introduced.

Within 10 years, with no more than a high school diploma, Erikson had been given appointments at Harvard, Yale, and the University of California at Berkeley. Again, he reflected on his lack of the "usual credentials" and the oddity of achieving positions at such elite institutions without them. Although he was urged to pursue a Ph.D. as a way of becoming more acceptable to the academic community, Erikson believed that he could learn more through his observations of children.

It was while he was at Berkeley that Erikson began his research into childhood among the Lakota and Hurok tribes. Although his work was rooted to a large extent in Freudian psychoanalytic assumptions and his own experience with psychoanalysis, Erikson was also influenced by the findings of Margaret Mead and other cultural anthropologists. Bringing together psychology with the social sciences, he developed his own strikingly original view of child development, in which society and culture play an important part in shaping children's psyches.

Whereas Freud's five stages of development covered only the first five years of life, Erikson elaborated a theory of lifelong development characterized by eight stages. He articulated this theory in his influential book *Childhood and Society,* published in 1950. In Erikson's view, each of the life stages contained its own vulnerability and its own potential, each decisive in personality formation and each building on the previous stage. He believed that normal development involved a series of "crises" that emerged predictably at various life stages, and that happiness depended on successful resolution of each crisis.

In contrast to the Freudians, Erikson saw the individual as very much a product of a specific culture. He was fascinated by the differences in the life stages and identity crises of young people growing up in different historical times or in markedly different environments, and this interest inspired him to write two acclaimed books of "psychohistory"—*Young Man Luther* (1958), which described Martin Luther's break with the Church in terms of the identity crisis, and *Gandhi's Truth* (1969), which received both the Pulitzer Prize and a National Book Award.

In the 1960s, Erikson became a professor of human development at

Harvard. His concepts of identity and the identity crisis gained currency in the popular culture of rebellion, while his claim that major psychological differences existed between women and men provoked a response from the emerging women's movement. The essays Erikson published in journals during those years were collected in two books, *Insight and Responsibility* (1964) and *Identity: Youth and Crisis* (1968).

After his retirement in 1970, Erikson continued to write and lecture, dividing his time between California and Massachusetts. He died in 1994 at the age of 91. Considered a "grand synthesizer," Erik Erikson left a body of work that continues to be read and discussed in multiple disciplines, including anthropology, biology, history, philosophy, medicine, and religion.

# JAMES MARK BALDWIN

Although his work was overlooked for decades, James M. Baldwin was a pioneer in the field of experimental psychology. Born in Columbia, South Carolina, in 1861, he spent his college years at Princeton, where he received a B.A. in 1884 and a Ph.D. in 1889. From Princeton, he moved to the University of Toronto, where he taught philosophy while he worked to establish a psychology laboratory for the university. The lab was a controversial venture, and Baldwin's appointment itself was controversial, as he was a follower of the German philosopher and psychologist Wilhelm Wundt—a groundbreaking thinker of the era.

Wundt's laboratory in Leipzig was the first in the world dedicated to experimental psychology, and his revolutionary approach, which used physiological techniques, was designed to move psychological study away from the domain of philosophy and toward the natural sciences. This was the psychology that interested Baldwin and the model that he worked to establish in his laboratory at the University of Toronto. However, in 1893, once the lab was in operation, he left Toronto for a position in psychology at Princeton, where he stayed until 1903. From Princeton, Baldwin moved on to teach philosophy and psychology at Johns Hopkins.

Baldwin's serious immersion in developmental work began with the birth of his first daughter in 1889 and his fascination with her behavior. When she was between the ages of 4 and 10 months, he conducted a series of experiments to study the process by which she learned to reach. In this series, he used precise methods and systematically controlled variables, such as the time of day, the color of objects placed in her path, their distance from her, and their position in relation to her.

Although his findings about infant reaching proved informative, the real value of Baldwin's work for an emerging psychological science was his attention to experimental design and his use of controlled, quantitative methods to focus on the development of a particular behavior. Moreover, as he observed his daughter's rapid cognitive development, he began to consider the relationship between imitation and volition in learning, and what he called "the genetic function of imitation," which moved him toward "a widened genetic view" of development. As he wrote in 1895, "No theory of development is complete . . . which does not account for the transmission in some way, from one generation to another, of the gains of the earlier generations, turning individual gains into [species] gains."

The theory that emerged from these insights first appeared in 1897, in his book *Social and Ethical Interpretations in Mental Development: A Study in Social Psychology,* awarded the Gold Medal of the Danish Academy of Sciences. In it, Baldwin articulated what was to become his most important theoretical legacy—the concept known as the *Baldwin effect* or *Baldwinian evolution*. In this theory, Baldwin noted that human behavioral decisions made and sustained across generations were indeed cultural practices. However, he proposed, they might also be considered adaptive and, in turn, among the factors that shape the human genome. Thus, he linked certain behaviors with a genetic advantage, a line of thought that places him at the heart of contemporary controversies in the fields of evolutionary developmental psychology and sociobiology.

Over the course of his career, Baldwin established two important journals: *Psychological Review* and *Psychological Bulletin*. He was also a founding member of the American Psychological Association and its sixth president. Between 1901 and 1905, he edited the three-volume *Dictionary of Philosophy and Psychology,* for which he solicited contributions from the leading figures in these fields at the turn of the twentieth century, and which led to his receiving Oxford University's first honorary doctorate of science.

In 1908, at the height of his career, Baldwin was arrested in a raid on a Baltimore bordello and forced to resign from Johns Hopkins. In the years that followed, he became an expatriate, dividing his time between Paris and Mexico, where he lectured at the National University in Mexico City. He died in Paris in November 1934.

Although he is not as well known as other giants in his field, Baldwin's ideas about experimentation, observation, and adaptive behaviors broke new ground and exerted a formative influence on later scholars, such as George Herbert Mead, Jean Piaget, Lev Vygotsky, and Lawrence Kohlberg (see Piaget, Vygotsky, and Kohlberg biographies).

# URI BRONFENBRENNER

Uri Bronfenbrenner was born in Moscow in 1917—the year of the Bolshevik Revolution in Russia. In 1918, four years of civil war began in his country. Bronfenbrenner left for the United States in 1923, at age 6. Perhaps because he had lived in a place and time of such dramatic disruption and change, Bronfenbrenner became particularly sensitive to the ways in which the environment affects the individual, a key idea in his theory of child development.

He earned his bachelor's degree from Cornell in 1938, with a double major in psychology and music, his M.A. from Harvard in developmental psychology, and his doctorate from the University of Michigan in 1942. Again experiencing the impact of his environment (the United States had entered World War II in 1941), Bronfenbrenner was inducted into the Army the day after he received his degree from Michigan. He served as a psychologist in the Air Corps and, later, in the U.S. Army Medical Corps. In 1948, he joined the faculty of Cornell, where he has remained ever since.

In his research, Bronfenbrenner focused on the interaction between the organism and its environment, and he came to view the developing person as embedded in a series of environmental systems. In his model, the developing child is nested not only within the family but also within school, community, societal, cultural, and national systems, all of which interact with one another and with the individual—a multilevel environment that is continually changing.

Moreover, each of these systems, or levels, is characterized by a set of roles, norms, and relationships. Bronfenbrenner asserted that development progresses most smoothly when the relations between the systems are compatible and when the expectations within each are similar. He called this *ecological systems theory,* then renamed it *bioecological systems theory* to emphasize the combined biological and environmental forces that together shape a child's development.

Describing the impact of multiple systems, Bronfenbrenner said, "We as a nation need to be reeducated about the necessary and sufficient conditions for making human beings human. We need to be reeducated not as parents—but as workers, neighbors, and friends; and as members of the organizations, committees, boards—and, especially, the informal networks that control our social institutions and thereby determine the conditions of life for our families and their children."

Before 1979, when he published his theory, social science fields each had separate specialties: For child psychologists, it was children; for anthropologists, culture; for sociologists, social institutions; for economists, the economy; for political scientists, government and policy; and so on. In contrast, Bronfenbrenner's model was interdisciplinary, highlighting interconnections between the fields. Thus, he transformed the study of humans and their environments.

But Bronfenbrenner was not only a theoretician. In 1965, he served on the planning committee that launched Head Start, a U.S. national school-readiness program designed to provide education, health, nutrition, and parent-involvement services to low-income children and their families. Bronfenbrenner convinced the committee that the program would be most effective if it involved the family and the community as well as the child. Parent involvement in school operations and administration was unheard of at the time, but it became a cornerstone of Head Start and a major contributor to its success.

More recently, he has focused on changes in American family life and the related concern that parents have less and less time to devote to their children. "Development," Bronfenbrenner said, "occurs through this process of progressively more complex exchanges between a child and somebody else—especially somebody who's crazy about that child." Moreover, he observes, the "human family is the most powerful, the most humane, and by far the most economical system known for making and keeping human beings human."

In 2004, Bronfenbrenner published *Making Human Beings Human: Bioecological Perspectives on Human Development,* a collection of essays that traces and summarizes his thoughts. "The main thesis of this volume," he writes in the introduction, "is that, to a greater extent than for any other species, human beings create the environments that shape the course of human development." Bronfenbrenner is widely regarded as one of the world's leading scholars in developmental psychology, child rearing, and human ecology—the interdisciplinary domain that he created.

# ESTHER THELEN

Esther Stillman Thelen was born in 1941 in Brooklyn, New York. She began her undergraduate education at Antioch College in Ohio and received her bachelor's degree from the University of Wisconsin, Madison. Her graduate work at the University of Missouri led to both a master's degree and a doctorate in biology, and she stayed on to work in the psychology department there from 1977 to 1985. Her next move was to Indiana University, where she joined the psychology department and remained for the rest of her career, teaching, conducting research, and training many scientists in her labs. In her teaching, Thelen stressed the importance of using a clear, compelling writing style for presenting scientific findings.

Thelen's research focused on the way babies develop early motor and mental skills, and the way those skills relate to each other and to the wider world. In short, she wanted to know how infants learn to control their bodies so they can interact with their environments.

"When a baby takes his or her first step," she said, "it looks as though the behavior just suddenly appeared. But actually the baby has been working on that problem for a year beforehand. So we want to start way before a baby can walk and try and track the components that go into walking."

With this goal in mind, Thelen watched babies as they discovered new skills and then tried to figure out how they did it—for example, how they went about reaching for objects or, on an even more specific level, how they learned to use their muscles and their hands, to contract them just the right amount, to calibrate the space, even to know where an object is.

Before Thelen's work became known, most scientists thought that babies progressed through relatively rigid stages, with walking and other physical advances corresponding with advances in certain brain regions. Her view, however, based in the dynamic systems perspective, was more complex. Through watching and recording, and by studying videotapes, she concluded that infants' accomplishments reflect an intricate and multifaceted interplay between the brain, the baby's growing awareness of his or her body, and the baby's environment.

Moreover, Thelen hypothesized, babies develop new skills as solutions to problems—for example, the problem of how to look at something intriguing, how to retrieve an interesting object, how to explore a new place or engage a new person. Also, she noted, while all normally developing babies eventually achieve the same milestones—for example, reaching with two hands, coordinating their limbs, walking, and developing gestures and speech—they get there in their own, sometimes circuitous, ways. Some babies, for example, skip the crawling stage and instead scoot on their bottoms before they move on to walking. Observing these variable pathways led Thelen to look beyond genetic programming to explain motor development.

"Dynamic systems theories depart from conventional approaches," she said, "because they seek to understand the overall behavior of a system not by dissecting it into parts but by asking how and under what circumstances the parts cooperate to produce a whole pattern." Said John Spencer, one of her colleagues, "She really viewed development at the level of the organism, the whole child, and showed that it's not just the genes or the brain but all these things coming together."

In addition to advancing scientists' understanding of children's overall development, Thelen's work has had an interdisciplinary impact—influencing kinesiology, cognitive science, computer science, robotics, and neuroscience. Her findings also had a major effect on physical therapy for babies and young children, prompting therapists to design individual exercises tailored to a child's body rather than using standard exercises for all children of a given age.

Thelen was a Fellow of the American Association for the Advancement of Science and the American Psychological Association, and president of the International Society for Infant Studies. When she died of cancer in 2004 at the age of 63, she was director of the Infant Motor Development Laboratory at Indiana University and president of the Society for Research in Child Development. Her husband, David Thelen, is a history professor at Indiana University, and she has two adult children.

# ELEANOR GIBSON

Eleanor Gibson was born Eleanor Jack in Peoria, Illinois, in 1910. She received both her bachelor's and master's degrees from Smith College. While she was an undergraduate there, she met James Gibson, her psychology professor, and the two married in 1932, the year after her graduation. Although romantic involvement between professor and student may be viewed as unorthodox, the marriage endured a lifetime, and the two psychologists occasionally collaborated in their research on perception. In 1938, Gibson received her doctorate in psychology from Yale University. While at Yale and after receiving her Ph.D., she taught at Smith College.

The Gibsons moved to Ithaca, New York, in 1949 so James could join the faculty of Cornell University. The school's antinepotism policy prevented Eleanor Gibson from also obtaining a teaching position there, so she worked as a research associate from 1949 to 1966. When the nepotism rule was changed in 1965, she joined the faculty of the psychology department—the first woman at Cornell to be appointed to an endowed professorship. Gibson stayed at Cornell until her retirement in 1979—the same year her husband died. Even after her retirement, she maintained an active career of writing and research.

Here is how Gibson described her research interests: "I was not attracted by Gestalt psychology and yearned for what I thought of as 'hard psychology.' I didn't like introspective methods. I wanted to be objective, as I thought of it then, and I wanted to work with animals and children." Specifically, she focused on the way the young learn to perceive their environment, and concluded that perception was an essentially adaptive process and that perceptual learning was a process of differentiation.

When Gibson was a young researcher, the general view was that human infants required a longer maturation period than the young of other species before they could perceive the simplest aspects of their surroundings. This view originated in part from the writing and thinking of the great philosopher and psychologist William James, but Gibson—

perhaps encouraged by her observations of her own young children—was both wise and bold enough to be skeptical. The story is told that her interest in children's ability to perceive was heightened during a trip the Gibson family took to the Grand Canyon. There, husband and wife debated whether they could safely let their 2-year-old daughter venture near the rim of the canyon.

The story does not go so far as to say who took which side of the debate or whose view prevailed, but once back at Cornell, Eleanor Gibson, with her colleague Richard Walk, put this question to scientific test. They constructed the famous "visual cliff" to investigate the process of depth perception—that is, of seeing objects in three dimensions. The image of the visual cliff, familiar to readers of introductory and developmental psychology texts worldwide, is described this way in a Cornell publication: "The picture shows a diapered infant, crawling across a checkerboard-patterned tabletop, toward its beckoning mother. Partway across the table, the checkerboard gives way to transparent glass, and although the infant could have continued safely, it has halted. . . . Her point was that depth perception and other skills for navigating a perilous world develop as needed—when locomotion is possible—and not before." She did similar experiments with animals, including rats and kittens. Later, she studied other perceptual skills as well—for example, how children learn to recognize and read words and how adults appreciate the sensory differences among wines.

Gibson's body of work led many to view her as a prime mover in the field of perceptual learning and as a driving force in constructing an ecological view of development in which infants and children are seen as explorers who actively seek information from their environments to guide their actions. Over the course of her career, she held academic appointments at the Center for Advanced Study in Behavioral Sciences in Palo Alto, California, the Massachusetts Institute of Technology, and several other universities. In 1992, President Bill Clinton awarded Eleanor Gibson the National Medal of Science, making her one of a very few psychologists to receive the nation's highest scientific honor. She died in December 2002 at the age of 92.

# DONALD O. HEBB

The great neuroscientist Donald Hebb was born in 1904 in Chester, Nova Scotia. As a young man, he hoped to become a novelist and believed that an understanding of human psychology would be key to achieving his vision. Although he was correct in his determination that as a fiction writer, he would need deep insight into human feelings and motivation, his study of psychology, first at Dalhousie University in Nova Scotia and then at McGill University in Montreal, Quebec, took him in an unexpected direction: toward science and the exploration of behavior based on the physiology of the nervous system.

In 1932, Hebb accompanied Karl Lashley, one of the most respected physiological psychologists of the time, to Cambridge, Massachusetts. At Harvard University, in 1936, Hebb completed his doctoral research on learning in animals and the role of early visual deprivation on perception. He returned to Canada to accept a fellowship at the Montreal Neurological Institute, where he investigated the impact of brain injury and surgery on human intelligence and behavior. At Queen's University in Kingston, Ontario, Hebb developed intelligence tests for both humans and animals, and his work in this area led him to conclude that experience played a greater role in determining intelligence than had often been assumed.

In 1942 Hebb rejoined Lashley, now director of the Yerkes Laboratories of Primate Biology in Florida. There, Hebb studied chimpanzee behavior—an experience that likely furthered his interest in the biological heritage of humans. He returned to McGill in 1946, and a year later became chair of the psychology department, where he remained for the rest of his teaching and research career, exploring the relationships between the mind, the brain, human learning, and human behavior.

In his research, Hebb collaborated with Wilder G. Penfield, a Canadian neurosurgeon who had become known for mapping functional areas of the human cerebral cortex and discovering that stimulating parts of the cortex could evoke memories, including memories of sounds and smells. Together, Hebb and Penfield worked on localizing memory in the brain, and they theorized that thoughts resulted from the activity of reverberating circuits of neurons called "cell assemblies."

Hebb's book, *The Organization of Behaviour*, published in 1949, became a key text in modern neuroscience. In it he proposed an idea that he called Hebb's postulate: "When an axon of cell A is near enough to excite a cell B and repeatedly or persistently takes part in firing it, some growth process or metabolic change takes place in one or both cells such that A's efficiency, as one of the cells firing B, is increased." In other words, he proposed that learning occurs within an organism through structural changes in the brain—more specifically, through the modification of synaptic connections between neurons due to repeated stimulation of receptors.

In the universities of that time, most psychology students expected to learn Freud's psychoanalytic perspective, with the goal of better understanding their own minds and those of the people around them. Instead, Hebb taught a biological approach to psychology that considered the role of both heredity and experience in human behavior.

Cognitive scientist Stevan Harnad describes his experience as one of Hebb's students in the early 1960s: "I realized what a radically different world view such a theory represented, and that it all had a ring of reality to it that made the Freudian notions I had been flirting with sound like silly fairy tales. Here were the real unconscious processes underlying our thinking." In a tribute to his former professor, Harnad articulates a second revelation he gained from Hebb: "that a theory need not be right in order to be informative and to guide us in the right direction." According to Harnad, Hebb saw his work as "pointing the way toward answers, rather than representing the answers themselves."

Hebb's landmark theories and his experiments on change in neural structures that accompanies learning foreshadowed neural network theory, an active line of research in artificial intelligence referred to as connectionism. His work has also inspired research on the effects of sensory deprivation and enrichment, brain plasticity, and the electrical and chemical pleasure centers in the brain.

Hebb was a Fellow of the Royal Society of London, recipient of over a dozen honorary degrees, and a laureate of the Canadian Medical Hall of Fame. Although he viewed B. F. Skinner as the greatest psychologist of the twentieth century, Hebb is himself regarded as having provided the real empirical alternative to behaviorism: cognitive science.

Hebb died in 1985 in Halifax, Nova Scotia. In honor of his work, today both the Canadian Psychological Association and the Canadian Society for Brain, Behaviour and Cognitive Science award prizes in his name for outstanding contributions to psychological science. Along with his many accomplishments, Hebb is remembered for his witty lectures, as seen in this representative quote: "A large brain, like large government, may not be able to do simple things in a simple way."

# JEAN PIAGET

Jean Piaget was born in 1896 in Neufchatel, Switzerland. An intellectually precocious child, he turned to the serious study of nature at an early age. Captivated by the birds, fossils, and marine life of the lakes of Switzerland, Piaget recorded his observations, publishing his first paper at age 10. By the time he was 15, he had published several papers on how the shell structures of the mollusk adapt to variations in the animal's habitat. These findings profoundly affected the way Piaget would eventually view the development of thinking. He saw change in cognitive structures as a special form of biological activity that was part of the overall process by which children gradually achieve a better adaptive fit with their surroundings.

Influenced by his godfather, Piaget developed an interest in philosophy, and especially in epistemology, which is concerned with the understanding of various forms of knowing. This early exposure to both biology and philosophy led Piaget, by his late teens, to become interested in biological explanations of the origins of knowledge.

Piaget completed his bachelor's degree at age 18 and his Ph.D. at age 21, both in the natural sciences. His interests in the empirical methods of psychology and in the study of children brought him to Zurich, where he worked in the clinic of the well-known psychoanalyst Bleuler. There, Piaget discovered the clinical method of psychoanalysis. A year later, when he went to work in the Paris laboratory of Alfred Binet and Theodore Simon, he quickly saw the importance of the clinical interview for understanding the thought processes of children. Asked to adapt English intelligence tests for French schoolchildren, he became fascinated by children's incorrect answers to test questions and the reasons for their mistakes, which seemed to follow predictable patterns related to age—an interest that would shape the course of his work.

At age 25, Piaget became Director of Research at the University of Geneva's Rousseau Institute, a center for the study of child psychology, where he remained for the rest of his career, devoting his energies to investigating the logic of children's thought. Through these efforts, Piaget became increasingly convinced of the differences between the thinking of children and that of adults. He began to view cognitive development in terms of movement through a series of stages—a sequence of qualitatively distinct reorganizations of thought over the course of childhood.

In the late 1930s and 1940s, drawing on careful observations of his three infant children, Piaget described how the infant's sensorimotor activity lays the groundwork for the thinking of childhood and adolescence. Motivated by these infant studies, Piaget revised his clinical interviewing methods and began devising tasks for children and adolescents in which they both acted on objects and engaged in conversation with an examiner about them. In the early 1940s, he published his work on children's understanding of physical quantities, number, and such physical concepts as distance, time, and speed. In the 1940s and 1950s, he devoted his energies to the educational implications of his theory and the study of adolescent thought. Many contemporary educational approaches—discovery learning, sensitivity to children's readiness to learn, and acceptance of individual differences—have their roots in the work of Piaget.

Piaget articulated four universal stages of cognitive development: sensorimotor, preoperational, concrete operational, and formal operational. As infants and children act on the environment, Piaget believed, specific psychological structures, or schemes, change through the exercise of two important intellectual functions: adaptation and organization. Over time, the exploratory behaviors of infants eventually transform into the abstract, logical intelligence of adolescence and adulthood.

Many recent studies suggest that infants display a variety of understandings earlier than Piaget believed. And new evidence indicates that cultural practices, schooling, and other aspects of social context profoundly affect Piagetian task performance. Today, experts widely agree that children's cognition is not as broadly stagelike as Piaget believed. Nevertheless, Piaget's contributions to the field of child development are gigantic—greater than those of any other theorist. In his 60-year career, he published scores of books and hundreds of articles. His work has stimulated a wealth of research into cognitive development and continues to inspire many new studies; his findings have served as the starting point for virtually every major contemporary perspective on cognitive development. Despite the inevitable criticisms and revisions of his ideas that have occurred as the study of child development and cognition has advanced, both psychologists and educators continue to recognize the tremendous importance of Piaget's theoretical and empirical contributions.

Research into cognitive development is far more fragmented today than it was when Piaget's ideas held sway. Investigators remain a long way from consensus on what to substitute for Piaget's theory. As noted researcher John Flavell pointed out, "Perhaps what the field needs is another genius like Piaget to show us how, and to what extent, all those cognitive-developmental strands within the growing child are knotted together."

# LEV VYGOTSKY

Lev Vygotsky was born into a Russian-Jewish family in 1896. Apparently, this was a good year for the field of human development, as the great cognitive-developmental theorist Jean Piaget was born in that same year (see Piaget biography). As a boy, Vygotsky was educated at home, instructed by a private tutor who conducted lessons using a method similar to the Socratic dialogue, with its emphasis on the clash of opposing viewpoints and their eventual resolution through synthesis. Vygotsky's concept of the zone of proximal development, which is central to his educational ideas, may have been rooted in these early experiences.

As an adolescent, Vygotsky attended first a public high school and then a selective private Jewish school. His brilliance and diverse abilities were evident to all of his teachers, but Vygotsky's special love was for the theater and poetry. His friends recalled that, in recitation, he would choose only those lines of a poem that he felt captured its essence. This approach seemed to give special significance to the role of condensed linguistic form in human cognition, an idea that would play an important role in Vygotsky's view of language and mind.

Vygotsky entered the University of Moscow not on the basis of his evident talent but, rather, by a stroke of luck, when he won a lottery that determined which Jewish students would be admitted to the best Russian universities. He graduated at age 21 with a firm grounding in history, philosophy, psychology, art, and literature (which remained his primary interest). Returning to his hometown of Gomel, he taught Russian and literature at vocational schools for tradesmen and teachers. He also began to read widely in psychology, which became his central interest. As a scholar of literature and a self-trained psychologist, Vygotsky brought a fresh, outsider's perspective to the field that may have contributed to his creative insights about human development.

In 1919, Vygotsky contracted tuberculosis, the disease that would eventually take his life. In 1924, after delivering an inspiring address at a national conference in psychology, the 28-year-old Vygotsky was named to an important research position at the Institute of Psychology in Moscow. There he worked feverishly to reorganize Russian psychology and to address serious social problems, such as illiteracy in Soviet society and difficulties in educating children with physical and mental disabilities.

The pace of Vygotsky's work accelerated in his final years. As his illness worsened, he refused hospitalization in favor of completing as many of his projects as possible. He died in 1934, when he was only 37. It was a time when Communist Party control over science and culture had tightened, and Vygotsky, among many others, was a target of Party criticism. Though his commitment to his theoretical ideas did not waver, he died anguished over being misunderstood by his contemporaries. Indeed, for 20 years after Vygotsky's death, his works were banned in the Soviet Union due to Stalinist repression. They began to be reissued in the 1950s and were first translated into English in the 1960s. As psychologists and educators encountered difficulty in fully verifying Piaget's stages, they turned to Vygotsky's sociocultural theory for help in understanding social and cultural influences on cognitive development.

Vygotsky's theory views children as active seekers of knowledge but also emphasizes the profound effect of social and cultural contexts on the way children's cognitive world is structured. Vygotsky believed that through joint activities with more mature members of society, children come to master activities and think in ways that have meaning in their culture. Further, he believed that children learn best when tasks are in their zone of proximal development—that is, in a range that the child cannot yet handle alone but can accomplish with the help of adults and more skilled peers.

Vygotsky was particularly interested in the way children use language to provide themselves with self-guidance and self-direction. Because language helps children think about their own behavior and select courses of action, he saw it as the foundation for all higher cognitive processes. In line with his emphasis on the vital role of both social experience and language in cognitive development, Vygotsky regarded make-believe play as a unique, broadly influential zone of proximal development in which children advance themselves as they try out a variety of challenging skills. In addition to stimulating a wealth of research on the contribution of social experiences to development, Vygotsky's theory has been influential in the field of education, where it is reflected in such approaches as assisted discovery, cooperative learning, and reciprocal teaching. In a new, Vygotsky-inspired educational approach, classrooms are transformed into communities of learners, where no distinction is made between adult and child contributions, and where both adults and children collaborate and develop.

# ROBBIE CASE

Robbie Case was born in 1944 in Barrie, Ontario, Canada, to a prosperous English-speaking family. He received a bachelor's degree in psychology from McGill University in Montreal in 1965, followed by a master's degree and a doctorate in educational theory from the University of Toronto.

In 1971, just after earning his Ph.D., Case was recruited to teach at the University of California, in Berkeley. Later, in 1988, he joined the faculty of Stanford University, also in California. Decker Walker, professor of education at Stanford, described Case as a sensitive teacher and noted that he was particularly attuned to his students and committed to helping them feel comfortable in the classroom.

When Case left Stanford, it was to return to Canada and the Ontario Institute for Studies in Education (OISE) at the University of Toronto. In 1993, he was made a fellow of the Canadian Institute for Advanced Research. Later, shortly after he was granted emeritus status, he became director of the University of Toronto's Institute of Child Study.

In his research and writing, Case focused on the way children think and on the ways their thinking patterns change with age and experience, specifically the gains they make in their capacity to process information. He is perhaps best known for helping to reexamine and transform Piaget's theory of cognitive development—work that he began at a time when few others were openly questioning Piaget's ideas (see Piaget biography). Case looked deeply into the minds of children, in hopes of offering a more precise account of their intellectual growth than Piaget had. What he achieved was a detailed picture of the way various cognitive structures interact and advance. As described by David Olson of the University of Toronto, Case's theories portrayed a process in which children's knowledge developed through stages of increasing complexity involving multiple operations embedded in hierarchies of structures.

But Case was not satisfied with doing pure research. He sought to go beyond *studying* children's development to *influence* it, especially the development of underprivileged children. Therefore, the field of education called to him, especially the domains of math and science. He believed that to succeed in these subjects, students must begin their academic careers with a strong intuitive sense of the nature of numbers, and he was one of the first to document the disparity between social classes in general number sense. In response, he developed a program in early mathematics designed to teach number sense rather than formal computations, with the objective of equalizing the performance of low-income and middle-income children. In doing this work, said David Olson, Case "showed that the growth of knowledge was not to be explained by generic properties such as intelligence or social class but by opportunities for learning."

Also working at the middle school and high school levels, Case identified concepts that were difficult for children of all social backgrounds and developed curriculum materials that worked with the learner's core intuitions. "It seems particularly important," he said, "to understand those successes that depend on intuition and creativity rather than just on the mastery of explicitly defined concepts and algorithms."

Over the course of his career, Case received numerous awards: a Guggenheim fellowship, a Van Leer Jerusalem fellowship, and a fellowship at the Stanford Center for Advanced Study in the Behavioral Sciences. His books on intellectual development have been translated into many languages, and symposia have been held in his honor by the University of Toronto, the American Educational Research Association, and the Society for Research in Child Development. Sadly, he was only 56 years old when he died in 2000, leaving behind his wife, Nancy, and three children.

Case's interest in seeing young people reach their full potential is embodied in the following quote: "Socialization is a process in which both the young and old have a stake. It serves many functions. One of the most important, however, is to enable the younger and less-experienced members of a culture to acquire the values, insights, and skills which are their heritage."

# HOWARD GARDNER

In part because of the fresh, broad-ranging view of intelligence that he articulated, Howard Gardner has had a significant effect on both education and psychology. He was born in 1943 in Scranton, Pennsylvania, the child of refugees from Nazi Germany—a fact that cannot have failed to mark his life and his aspirations. As a boy, he was both an excellent student and a promising pianist. Although he stopped his piano lessons as he approached adolescence, the arts, music, and teaching have remained important themes throughout his career.

The first in his family to attend college, Gardner went to Harvard to study history, with the thought of a career in law. Once at college, however, he had the opportunity to study with psychoanalyst Erik Erikson (see Erikson biography) and psychologist Jerome Bruner, who was a key figure in cognitive psychology and educational reform. The ideas and teachings of these two professors drew Gardner toward an interest in the social sciences, and he graduated in 1965 with a bachelor's degree in social relations. After a year at the London School of Economics, Gardner decided to continue graduate studies at Harvard, where he received his Ph.D. in developmental psychology in 1971.

As a new psychologist, Gardner set out to study children and their artistic abilities, but after he attended a lecture given by Norman Geschwind, a well-known neuropsychologist, his interest once again shifted, this time to neuropsychology. As a result, Gardner began working with Geschwind on a long series of studies on cognitive problems in people suffering brain damage.

In 1983, in *Frames of Mind,* Gardner pulled together many of his ideas on human cognition. In this book, he set out his theory of multiple intelligences, challenging the notion that humans have a single intelligence that can be assessed by standard IQ tests. Instead, Gardner asserted, individuals have a broad range of human capacities, or intelligences, that are relatively autonomous. These include some aptitudes that had not traditionally been considered intellectual and not even cognitive—for example, musical and interpersonal intelligence.

In the 1980s, Gardner moved from theory and research toward a more applied focus, concerned particularly with issues of teaching, learning, and school reform, and in 1986, he became a professor of cognition and education at the Harvard Graduate School of Education, where Lawrence Kohlberg also taught (see Kohlberg biography). Then, with Harvard colleagues, Gardner founded Project Zero, a group whose mission was to "understand and enhance learning, thinking, and creativity in the arts, as well as humanistic and scientific disciplines, at the individual and institutional levels."

Although Gardner's theory of multiple intelligences has not yet been firmly grounded in research, educators in many parts of the world have applied it in the areas of curriculum, pedagogy, and assessment. Gardner has pushed for recognition of the full range of human capacities, for teaching methods that stimulate imaginative capacities, for institutional settings that encourage creativity and arts education, and for assessment methods that acknowledge many forms of critical and creative thinking. In particular, during the past two decades, Gardner and his colleagues at Project Zero have been designing performance-based tests and using the theory of multiple intelligences to create more individualized teaching and testing methods.

In a 1997 interview, Gardner said: "I see the purpose of education as helping people understand the best answers that cultures and societies have come up with to basic questions. . . . So at the end we can form our own personal answers to those questions, which will be based to a significant extent on how other people have approached them, and will at the same time allow us to make our own syntheses." In recent collaborative research, Gardner has examined the relationship between a person's exemplary work and his or her personal values, and in a recent book, *Changing Minds,* he examines the processes by which individuals change their own minds and the minds of others.

Gardner has received numerous awards, including a MacArthur Fellowship in 1981, the Grawemeyer Award in Education in 1990, and a Guggenheim Fellowship in 2000. He is also the recipient of honorary degrees from universities in Italy, Ireland, Israel, and Canada, among others.

"I want my children to understand the world," said Gardner, "but not just because the world is fascinating and the human mind is curious. I want them to understand it so that they will be positioned to make it a better place."

# FRASER MUSTARD

Although trained as a physician, Fraser Mustard has become a leader in Canadian efforts to understand the effects of socioeconomic factors on health and human development, and especially, to promote early childhood health and welfare.

Mustard was born, raised, and educated in Toronto. He began his college education at the University of Toronto in engineering but, after one year, switched to medicine, graduating in 1953. He went on to receive a Ph.D. in biology from Cambridge University in England, where he studied hematology and blood disorders. After his return to Toronto in 1956, he held a series of research positions at such institutions as the University of Toronto and McMaster University in Hamilton, Ontario, where he helped establish a new school of medicine and health sciences.

In 1982, Mustard left McMaster to found the Canadian Institute for Advanced Research (CIAR) in Toronto. The purpose of the institute was to assemble distinguished thinkers from across Canada and the world, and to provide them with research time and networking opportunities to respond to scientific and social challenges. Over the years, CIAR researchers, working in interdisciplinary teams, have tackled a range of issues relating to the natural world and human society, such as: "What makes some countries wealthy and others poor?" "How did genes and organisms evolve, and how rapidly do environmental changes lead to modifications in the genome?" "How do early experiences affect biological systems and, thereby, set the course of subsequent development?" Knowledge generated by the institute is applied around the world.

In the mid-1990s, Mustard was invited to make a presentation to the Ontario Conservative caucus. There, he described the profound effects that technological, social, and economic changes were having on families and children. A few years later, the Canadian premier, remembering Mustard's earlier presentation, sought his advice on issues related to early childhood development. Thus began the Early Years Study, which Mustard conducted with Margaret McCain to assess the status of

Ontario's children and make recommendations on how best to nurture them.

In the resulting report, entitled "Reversing the Real Brain Drain," Mustard and McCain drew from neuroscience, developmental psychology, social sciences, anthropology, epidemiology, and other disciplines to explore the relationships between early brain development and an individual's learning, behavior, and health throughout the lifespan. Findings demonstrated the powerful, long-lasting influence of early social and physical environments on development. The report concluded that Ontario could do better for its young people, "and that to improve the early years for young children will require the commitment of all citizens from all sectors in Ontario, its government and the media."

Among other things, Mustard and McCain recommended establishing a network of early child development and parenting centers, tax incentives for developing the centers, improved maternity and parental leave benefits, family-friendly workplaces, and a network for community information sharing. The report also argued that a sensitive period exists for brain development, and that the wiring and sculpting of neurons during the early years lay a foundation for competence and coping skills throughout life. Moreover, Mustard and McCain noted, the brain is most malleable during infancy and early childhood; therefore, that is the time for offering the most effective interventions.

The government embraced the report and began to implement it, but three years later, in a follow-up report in 2002, Mustard and McCain concluded that the effort had fallen short. They estimated that of Ontario's 900,000 preschool children, 212,000 were still at risk for learning, behavior, and health problems later in life. Mustard and McCain called for a network of early childhood development and parenting centers for all families with young children, not just those in the lower socioeconomic brackets. Further, the report estimated the cost of building a network of centers to cover all preschool children. "This may seem like a large sum of money for a government focused on cutting taxes," Mustard and McCain wrote, "but for governments that are vitally interested in the quality of human capital and the future of their society, it is a small sum of money for a wealthy society such as Ontario."

One Canadian business executive summed up Mustard's thinking this way: "If you want an idea of what your economy will look like in say 15 or 20 years . . . if you want an economy that's vibrant, citizens who are productive and a workplace that's innovative—think about the investment you're making in very young people today." Accordingly,

Mustard advocates cooperation among systems of education, economy, and health care through pooling of resources and knowledge—a proposal aimed at breaking down barriers to optimum human development.

Mustard has received numerous awards for his work, including the Companion of the Order of Canada, the Order of Ontario, and the Gairdner Foundation International Award for Medical Research. He is a consultant with UNICEF and the World Bank on issues related to child development. An inductee to the Canadian Medical Hall of Fame, Mustard currently leads the Founders' Network, which links individuals in the private and public sectors in Canada and other countries to maintain support for CIAR. He is also a member of the Centre of Excellence of Early Child Development; a member of the board of directors of Beatrice House, a residential program for homeless mothers and their children; and Chairperson Emeritus of the newly incorporated Council for Early Child Development.

# ELIZABETH BATES

Elizabeth Bates was born in 1947 in Wichita, Kansas. She received her B.A. in psychology from St. Louis University in 1968 and her doctorate in human development from the University of Chicago in 1974. During her college years, she traveled extensively and adventurously—on a motorcycle through Nicaragua and Latin America, and later in Europe. She spent a year in Rome at the American University, where she developed deep ties, and she became fluent in Spanish, Italian, and French. Not surprisingly, perhaps, she made language the central concern of her research and writing—in particular, how language is acquired, how it is organized, how it can be lost, and how the brain is organized to process it.

In the 1960s and early 1970s, when Bates was a student, the thinking of Noam Chomsky dominated the understanding of language acquisition. In Chomsky's view, language was a system that was unique to the human species and grounded in a single set of rules that applied to all languages. Bates, however, believed that the truth lay elsewhere. For example, she pointed out that most research on language had been done in English, so any speculation about universals was weak. And on the basis of her fluency in several languages, she contended that linguistic differences did indeed affect language acquisition. Through the years, she and Chomsky sparred over these ideas.

In 1975, with Italian colleagues, Bates published a paper on the relevance of gestures in the emergence of language—a topic that remained a central interest in her research. Then, in 1977, she published her first book, *Language and Context,* a study of Italian-speaking children, highlighting the connections between the practical rules children learn for language use (pragmatics) and the context in which that language is acquired. Also during the 1970s, pursuing her interest in language differences, she worked with colleagues to establish an international network of researchers for collaboration on cross-linguistic comparisons.

In 1981, Bates joined the faculty of the University of California, San Diego, first in psychology, then as a founding member of the world's first cognitive science department, exploring the development of language and its neural, cognitive, and social components. In 1983, she began her study of aphasia, a language impairment resulting from brain injury. In these studies, she discovered that patients' communication deficits varied depending on the language they spoke, which again undermined the notion of universals.

From her varied projects, Bates developed a general theory that linguistic knowledge is distributed throughout the brain, rather than in a single center for language development. Moreover, she found that young children with injury to the language areas of the brain could still develop normal language abilities—thus demonstrating the brain's flexibility, or *plasticity,* in learning language. And she came to view language as intricately linked with evolutionarily ancient nonlinguistic skills. Pulling the many threads together, she theorized that characteristics of the world's languages determine the way the brain organizes language-related information and incorporates it during development and in cases of disease.

In addition to being a theorist and an active empirical scientist, Bates created several important tools for cognitive scientists. These include the MacArthur Communicative Development Inventory, which has versions in 35 languages and is one of the most widely used tools for assessing communicative development; the International Picture Naming Project, an effort that has generated developmental and behavioral data on action and object naming in seven languages; and, most recently, Voxel-Based Lesion–Symptom Mapping (VLSM), a brain-imaging technique used to correlate sites of brain lesions with degree of behavioral deficits in patients who have brain damage. This last contribution was particularly exciting for Bates, who described it as "an important breakthrough . . . a bridge between two different traditions in brain research—lesion–behavior mapping and functional magnetic resonance imaging (fMRI)."

In December 2003, not long after she made her comments on VLSM, Bates died of pancreatic cancer at age 56. Bereft friends and colleagues praised her ability to master diverse fields and to both discover and develop bridges across topics as she had moved ever closer to a unified view of language, cognition, and the brain. She had been a gifted teacher and mentor as well. Said Fred Dick, a former student, "She made us think harder, write more, write better, and argue with more passion." And another, Nina Dronkers, described her this way: "She was not afraid to be different or to teach her students to think for themselves and to stand up for their own ideas. In doing so, she provided enormous support to those of us less courageous than she and gave us confidence and encouragement to stand up and say what we needed to say."

# JEROME KAGAN

Jerome Kagan was born in Newark, New Jersey, in 1929. He earned his undergraduate degree from Rutgers University, his master's degree from Harvard, and, in 1954, his Ph.D. in psychology from Yale. Three years later, he took a position as a research associate at the Fels Research Institute in Yellow Springs, Ohio.

The institute, founded in 1929, sponsored the Fels Longitudinal Study, an effort to assess the effects of the Great Depression on child development and to explore the question of why people differ from one another. In the 1950s, Kagan's task was to track personality traits and the effects of parenting styles, and this research led to his first book, *Birth to Maturity* (1962), a study of the degree to which humans carry personality traits from infancy and childhood to adolescence and beyond. This theme, along with an interest in developmental influences and variations, have had ongoing prominence in his work.

In the mid-1960s, for example, Kagan lived in a Guatemalan village, where he studied the relationship between children's biological characteristics, the cultural influences they experienced, and their cognitive development. Drawing comparisons with American children, he concluded that children's biology promotes a regular developmental progression even under unfavorable circumstances.

In 1964, Kagan joined the faculty at Harvard, where he remains today as Daniel and Amy Starch Professor of Psychology and director of the Mind/Brain/Behavior Interfaculty Initiative, an interdisciplinary program that aims to "elucidate the structure, function, evolution, development, and pathology of the nervous system in relation to human behavior and mental life."

At Harvard, Kagan's research has focused on the cognitive and emotional development of children during the first decade of life, with a special concern for inherited temperamental dispositions and the role that temperament plays in personality and moral emotions. He has also explored the differences between inhibited and uninhibited children, tracking their development from infancy to adolescence.

Like many important thinkers and scientists before him, Kagan has taken unpopular positions and provoked extensive debate. For example, his research has reintroduced physiology as a determinant of psychological characteristics—a highly controversial position at a time when many developmental psychologists emphasize the power of the environment in shaping the individual. "In particular," wrote a reporter for the *Boston Globe* in 2004, "he's caused some backs to stiffen with his staunch rejection of 'attachment theory'—the idea, pioneered after World War II by British psychiatrist John Bowlby [on the basis of his studies of children who had experienced early, prolonged separation from their mothers], that the bond between mother and infant, as measured in the first year, plays a key role in later emotional and even intellectual growth."

Kagan has also challenged Mary Ainsworth's research on attachment and, in particular, the Strange Situation (see Ainsworth biography): "Some children," Kagan said, "are born with a temperament that makes them very vulnerable to becoming terrified when their mother leaves them alone in an unfamiliar place. And they're so upset that when the mother returns, it's very difficult for her to soothe the child, not because of the attachment but because this is a temperamentally fearful child."

Similarly controversial has been Kagan's effort to broaden the frame of environmental influences on the child's development. For example, in his most recent book, *Three Seductive Ideas,* he challenges the wide-spread belief that parenting and other experiences during the first years of a child's life are the most important determinants of adult personality. "What's happening after infancy," he said in a radio interview in 2000, "the neighborhood you live in, the quality of school you go to, the recognition that you belong to an economically advantaged or economically disadvantaged group, those factors have much more power on your future dignity, job, happiness, than what's happened to you in the first two years of life." In short, he continued, "It's not that early experience has no effect, but it doesn't fix it the way you fix a photograph or a piece of film."

In addition to publishing extensively, Kagan has won numerous awards, including the Hofheimer Prize of the American Psychiatric Association and the Distinguished Scientist Award of the American Psychological Association. He has served on numerous committees of the National Academy of Sciences, on the President's Science Advisory Committee, and on the Social Science Research Council.

# MARY AINSWORTH

Mary Salter Ainsworth was born in Glendale, Ohio, in 1913. When she was a young child, her family moved to Toronto, where she lived for many years. At age 15, she read William McDougall's book *Character and the Conduct of Life,* and the realization that people could look within themselves to understand their own feelings and behavior, rather than seeking external causes, inspired her to pursue a career as a psychologist. She majored in psychology as an undergraduate at the University of Toronto and continued her graduate studies there, receiving a Ph.D. in developmental psychology in 1939.

During her undergraduate years, the "security theory" of Ainsworth's mentor, William Blatz, captured her attention and eventually served as the basis for her doctoral dissertation. The dissertation contained the first reference to the "secure base"—the idea that the family provides a foundation from which children can explore new skills and interests.

In 1942, Ainsworth enlisted in the Canadian Women's Army Corps and attained the rank of major. A subsequent interest in clinical psychology flowed from two service positions she held while in the Women's Army Corps—one, supervising women's rehabilitation. After leaving the army, she returned to the University of Toronto, where she taught personality psychology and conducted research.

After marrying in 1950, Ainsworth moved to London with her husband. There, she had the good fortune to work in John Bowlby's research group at the Tavistock Institute. Bowlby was a child psychiatrist whose research focus was the damage that accompanies mother–child separation, and working with him meshed well with Ainsworth's interest in security theory. Also at the Tavistock Institute, Ainsworth was exposed to the techniques of naturalistic observation and to the theory that infant–mother attachment has a biological foundation.

In 1954, Ainsworth accompanied her husband to Uganda, where, with the ideas she had been exploring at the Tavistock Institute fresh in her mind, she obtained funding for a study of mother–infant separation at the East African Institute for Social Research. Because the separation study was not feasible, she switched her focus to observing patterns of infant–mother attachment in the homes of Ugandan women. Here, she recognized the relevance of Bowlby's ideas on the biological roots of attachment, and the work that came out of Ainsworth's Ugandan study in turn influenced Bowlby as he reformulated and further developed attachment theory.

Late in 1954, the Ainsworths moved to Baltimore, and Mary taught at Johns Hopkins while also conducting a small private practice in diagnostic assessment, especially with children. In 1961, she began the groundbreaking Baltimore Study, a close look at infant–mother attachment during the first year of life. The Baltimore Study became known for its intensive, detailed home observations, recorded as moment-by-moment narratives, noting many aspects of the mother–infant relationship: feeding, close body contact, face-to-face play, and crying.

During her years at Johns Hopkins, and later on the faculty of the University of Virginia, Ainsworth continued to focus on attachment research, proposing that the theory might be extended to friendship, mentor, and spousal relationships. In addition, she supervised many graduate students, who continued to extend and expand her work with their own research and publications on attachment theory. From 1984 until her death in 1999, she was professor emerita at the University of Virginia. During her long career, Ainsworth published many journal articles and books, including *Child Care and the Growth of Love* (1965) and *Patterns of Attachment* (1978). She was also the recipient of many awards, including the Gold Medal for Scientific Contributions of the American Psychological Foundation, which she received in 1998.

Ainsworth is most widely known for devising the "Strange Situation," a technique for assessing attachment quality in the laboratory by observing differences in infants' reactions to a series of separations from and reunions with their mothers. But her impact on the field of developmental psychology is far broader. Major contributions include the concept of the secure base, her pioneering work in methodology with naturalistic home observations, the multicultural perspective inherent in the work she did in Uganda, and the patterns of infant–mother attachment that she formulated. Ainsworth's work has also filtered into many homes, altering parenting practices—particularly as a result of her finding that responding sensitively to an infant's distress leads to less crying and a more harmonious relationship between baby and caregiver.

# LAWRENCE KOHLBERG

Lawrence Kohlberg, best known for his work on moral development, was born in 1927 to a wealthy family in Bronxville, New York. As a graduate of Phillips Academy, an elite private high school, young Kohlberg left this privileged setting to follow an unconventional path: He became a crew member on a freighter that was smuggling Jewish World War II refugees into Palestine—a decision that speaks volumes about his sense of moral purpose and his own level of moral development.

Following this experience, in 1948, Kohlberg was prepared to continue his formal education. He enrolled at the University of Chicago, but he scored so well on admissions tests that he placed out of most course requirements and received his bachelor's degree in one year. Staying on at Chicago for graduate work in psychology, he began the research that would define his career. He interviewed children and adolescents about moral issues by posing his famous "Heinz dilemma"—a hypothetical situation that pits the value of obeying the law (not stealing) against the value of human life (saving a dying person)—and then exploring the reasoning behind their responses. Kohlberg's doctoral dissertation, published in 1958, set out the three levels and six stages of moral development for which he became well known. His use of empirical methods to explore questions of morality brought attention to his work.

In 1968, at age 40, Kohlberg joined the faculty of the Harvard Graduate School of Education. There, the events of the era—the Vietnam War and the civil rights and women's movements—shaped his experience and his continuing interest in moral questions, as students sought direct answers to their own political and moral dilemmas about how to address the injustices they saw around them.

Piaget's theories of moral development had stimulated Kohlberg's interest in the subject, and Kohlberg then extended Piaget's work, following the development of moral judgment into adulthood (see Piaget biography). Kohlberg also went beyond the psychoanalytic and behaviorist views, in which adults impose morality on children and moral development is largely limited to early childhood. As Jerome Kagan, a colleague at Harvard, put it, in contrast to the psychoanalytic position, "Larry helped developmental psychologists to understand that a child's moral development doesn't spring forth fully developed at three or four years old" (see Kagan biography).

To Kohlberg, the child was "a moral philosopher" who—moved by social relationships and a variety of emotions, including love, respect, and empathy—generated his or her own moral codes. Moreover, Kohlberg hypothesized, as children encounter moral difficulties, they become motivated to further develop their moral thinking. Likewise, as their intelligence and ability to interact with others improve, so do their patterns of moral reasoning.

At the center of moral development, according to Kohlberg, is discussion. That is, by discussing moral dilemmas and encountering cognitive conflicts, children could come to see the reasonableness of more advanced moral thought and develop greater flexibility of judgment. In this way, he believed, formal education could promote moral development. And he sought to put his theories into practice by encouraging the formation of democracies, or "just communities," in schools and prisons. His belief was that moral education would flourish in an environment in which everyone had decision-making power.

No discussion of Kohlberg would be complete without reference to Carol Gilligan, who became perhaps the best known questioner of Kohlberg's theories when she asserted that his research had "ignored some vast cultural silences" by excluding the voices of women and people of color. Despite her differences with him, however, Gilligan credits Kohlberg and his work with drawing her back to the field of psychology at a time when she had practically abandoned it. Said Gilligan, "I remember his courage, his determination to talk about moral values in psychology, his bravery in countering the claim that psychology was a value-neutral social science."

In 1971, while doing cross-cultural work in Belize, Kohlberg became ill with a parasitic infection that he struggled with for the rest of his life. As described in a Harvard Graduate School of Education news article about his life and legacy, "Toward the very end, Kohlberg was disheveled, even distraught. While on a day pass from a local hospital on January 19, 1987, Kohlberg drove to Winthrop, parked his car on a dead-end street, and plunged into the sea." His body was later recovered from Boston Harbor. Although his findings and theories went in and out of favor during the course of his lifetime, his vision and approach continue to have a profound impact on the field of human development.

# ALBERT BANDURA

Albert Bandura was born in 1925 in a small town in northern Alberta, Canada. Growing up in this one-school hamlet with few teachers and few teaching resources, Bandura gained what he later described as self-directedness. This quality served him well in his career and would influence his theories of human behavior. His choice of psychology as a field of study at the University of British Columbia, however, came about by chance when he had an opening in his college schedule that a psychology course would fill. Three years later, he graduated with an award in psychology and went on to graduate school at the University of Iowa. Years later, he wrote about the fact that he had found his path to psychology by chance, using this personal experience to illustrate how individuals can create new circumstances and opportunities for themselves. Chance played a role in Bandura's personal life as well. One Sunday in the 1950s, he went to meet a friend at a golf course, but because he was late, he crossed paths with Virginia Varns, who became his wife and lifelong partner.

While Bandura was at the University of Iowa, most researchers in the psychology department viewed human development as a learning process that occurred through direct conditioning. Bandura disagreed with the emphasis that other theories placed on trial-and-error learning—he had other ideas about how learning might occur. He conjectured that vicarious experiences also contributed to social learning and suggested that people could learn by watching others. At Stanford, where he joined the faculty in 1953, he began field studies of social learning and aggression, with a special interest in the role of observation and modeling in human behavior. Specifically, Bandura wanted to explain aggressive behavior in boys who came from advantaged communities. His field research led him to conclude that aggressive adolescents often had parents who exhibited aggressive attitudes, and he hypothesized that children might behave aggressively because they model their behavior after aggressive adults.

Bandura moved his investigations of observational learning into the laboratory, and this led to his famous study using the inflatable Bobo doll, in which he investigated children's responses to observing violent models. The research confirmed his hypothesis that children could learn new patterns of behavior through observation and modeling, in the absence of reinforcement. This position moved him away from the dominant theories of the time. It was also inconsistent with the Freudian theory of catharsis, which suggested that watching aggressive models would actually decrease the observer's aggressive drives and behavior. Bandura's early Bobo doll research was a seminal influence on current investigations addressing the impact of aggressive models in the media on children's development.

In other lines of research, Bandura concluded that learners not only imitate what they see, but extract rules that underlie modeled behavior, thus gaining the flexibility to go beyond what they witness. In many senses, Bandura himself had demonstrated this capacity by moving beyond existing theories about the learning process. This view of human adaptability allows for creativity in the learning process; Bandura believed that while experience affects learning, humans can, in addition, direct their own behavior.

In the 1960s, Bandura began a program of research on the development of self-regulation in children. Consistent with his emphasis on self-direction, he theorized that people were capable of regulating their own motivation and behavior through the delivery of self-reward and delayed reinforcement. During the 1970s and 1980s at Stanford University, Bandura investigated the relationships between motivation, behavior, and self-regulation and formulated his social-cognitive theory of human functioning. In this fresh, groundbreaking view, people function as agents within a mix of personal, behavioral, and environmental influences, organizing and regulating their behavior by creating their own positive and negative consequences. Key to this theory is the human capacity for symbolic thought. The ability to represent environment and experiences symbolically allows people to reflect on their own behavior, plan for the future, and choose courses of action.

Bandura's long list of honorary degrees and awards includes the Lifetime Achievement Award from the Association for the Advancement of Behavior Therapy in 2001 and the Outstanding Lifetime Contribution to Psychology Award from the American Psychological Association in 2004. Moreover, his social-cognitive theory continues to thrive today, with broad applicability in settings as diverse as education, sports, health, medicine, mental health, and organizations. Concerned with how scientific knowledge influences society, Bandura sits on many congressional committees and advisory boards, and assists federal agencies in using his research findings to improve the human condition.

# ELEANOR MACCOBY

Eleanor Emmons Maccoby was born in 1917 in Tacoma, Washington. She was the second of four daughters in a family who were quite unusual for that era: They were vegetarians who were interested in Eastern thought and religion as well as astrology, occult phenomena, and ESP. Maccoby, however—after testing the validity of ESP in her earliest psychology experiment—became a skeptic about the mystical arts. This skepticism, perhaps, was the soil from which her scientific rigor and thinking grew.

At Reed College, which she attended for two years, Maccoby was exposed to a strongly behaviorist perspective. She then transferred to the University of Washington, where she majored in psychology and was influenced by the stimulus–response learning theory of her teachers.

In 1940, after graduation, she moved with her husband, Nathan Maccoby, to Washington, D.C., where she worked as a study director for the Division of Program Surveys of the U.S. Department of Agriculture (USDA). At the USDA, Maccoby studied topics ranging from consumer income and savings to the postwar experiences of veterans suffering from what is now known as posttraumatic stress disorder. And she acquired experience with field-interview studies—skills she would continue to use throughout her career.

Maccoby left the USDA for graduate work at the University of Michigan, where she studied traditional learning theory and served as study director in the Survey Research Center. Another move took her to Boston; there, in the Harvard lab of B. F. Skinner, she completed her dissertation research—a conditioning study with pigeons that was grounded in traditional learning theory.

After receiving her Ph.D., Maccoby began to teach in Harvard's Department of Social Relations, an interdisciplinary department where she encountered the perspectives of anthropologists and sociologists as well as clinical and social psychologists. When Robert Sears established the Laboratory on Human Development at Harvard, Maccoby was invited to participate in a large-scale study of child-rearing practices and their relation to young children's personality development. Her role was to manage interviews with mothers about their parenting values and behaviors; this experience, too, helped shape her career, as she has since published extensively on the topic of child rearing.

In 1953, Sears left Harvard, and Maccoby began teaching his child psychology and child development courses. This new challenge solidified her identity as a developmental psychologist. Maccoby, who had never before studied child psychology, would later say, "I underwent an ideological change in the course of studying Piaget and other child development literature. I was ready for the cognitive revolution that occurred in the 1950s" (see Piaget biography).

In 1958, Maccoby and her husband were invited to teach at Stanford for a year. Once there, both were offered permanent faculty positions—she in the Department of Psychology, where she has remained for the rest of her career, moving further from the behaviorist influences of her graduate education.

Maccoby's main interests have been in children's development in relation to family functioning and parenting methods. She has also investigated the impact of changes in family structure. In a longitudinal study of children of divorce begun in the 1980s, she looked at the impact of custody arrangements on children's adjustment. Another major focus, beginning in the 1970s and continuing to the present, has been the importance of gender in children's spontaneous social groupings and the implications of gender segregation in children's peer relationships for adult life. Additional areas of interest have included the influence of television on children's use of time, the effect of family patterns on first-time voting behavior, and selective listening and selective attention.

While advancing the depth and reach of developmental psychology, Maccoby also managed to rear three children. Describing the challenges of combining work and family, she said, "When my children were young, I worked part time so I could take care of them. My teaching load remained the same, but I gave up doing research, and there was a five- to six-year period when I didn't publish much. The balancing act is never easy. I handled it by managing my schedule somewhat creatively. I . . . [got] up at 2:00 a.m. and worked until 4:00 a.m. With no distractions, I managed to be quite productive. And this worked better for me than to try to work late into the evening after I had fed my kids and put them to bed. I continued this middle-of-the-night shift for 20 years."

The result of Maccoby's discipline and dedication is a body of research focused on some of the most important issues in human development: the parent's role in the process of socialization, the development of gender differences, and the long-term impact of divorce. Her work has led to a more complex understanding of the processes of social and personality development and, especially, of the multiplicity of influences on the developing child.

Maccoby has received many honors, including, in 1996, the American Psychological Foundation's Gold Medal Award for Life Achievement in the Science of Psychology. As developmental psychologist Laura Berk put it, Maccoby's continuing leadership in part flows from the knowledge that when a major dispute arises in the field—such as the question, "Does parenting matter?"—she can muster a strong case and argue it incisively.